☆ ☆ ☆

Franklin Pierce

Franklin Pierce

John DiConsiglio

AMERICA'S
14TH
PRESIDENT

Children's Press®
A Division of Scholastic Inc.
New York / Toronto / London / Auckland / Sydney
Mexico City / New Delhi / Hong Kong
Danbury, Connecticut

Library of Congress Cataloging-in-Publication Data

DiConsiglio, John.
     Franklin Pierce / by John DiConsiglio.
       p. cm. — (Encyclopedia of presidents. Second series)
     Summary: A biography of the fourteenth president of the United States,
with information on his childhood, family, political career, presidency, and
legacy.
Includes bibliographical references (p.) and index.
  ISBN 0-516-24235-0
   1. Pierce, Franklin, 1804–1869—Juvenile literature. 2. Presidents—United
States—Biography—Juvenile literature. [1. Pierce, Franklin, 1804–1869.
2. Presidents.] I. Title. II. Series.
E432.D53 2003
973.6'6'092—dc22   2003015942

CHILDREN'S PRESS and associated logos are trademarks and or registered
trademarks of Scholastic Library Publishing. SCHOLASTIC and associated
logos are trademarks and or registered trademarks of Scholastic Inc.
1 2 3 4 5 6 7 8 9 10 R 13 12 11 10 09 08 07 06 05 04

Contents

Inauguration Day, 1853

On a bitter cold and windswept afternoon in March of 1853, Franklin Pierce stood outside the east portico of the U.S. Capitol in Washington, D.C. Flakes of snow dusted his curly hair, the first signs of a snowfall that would soon blanket the city. Standing before Supreme Court chief justice Roger Taney, Pierce placed his hand on a law book, becoming the only president before or since who did not place his hand on a Bible. Then he was sworn in as the 14th president of the United States.

Pierce stepped up to the speaker's podium. Without notes, he began speaking with a strong voice, one that admirers compared to a trumpet. Yet his mood was as gray as the Washington weather. "It is a relief to feel that no heart but my own can know the personal regret and bitter sorrow over which I have been borne to a position so suitable for others, rather than desirable for myself," he began. Later in the speech, he said, "You have summoned me in my weakness. You must sustain me with your strength."

Perhaps no president has ever taken office in such sad circumstances. Just two months before his inauguration, Pierce, his wife Jane, and their eleven-year-old son Benjamin were traveling by train from Boston to their home in Concord, New Hampshire. Benjamin, nicknamed "Benny," was their pride and joy.

Then suddenly, the train jumped its tracks. The car the Pierces were in tipped over and slid down an embankment, throwing passengers from their seats. Others in the car were injured, but one passenger was killed—young Benny Pierce.

The death of their son devastated the new president and first lady. Two infant sons had died earlier, one soon after birth and the other at the age of four. Now they had lost their only remaining child. Jane came to believe that the disaster was a sign from God that Pierce should never have run for president. Two months later, she refused to attend her husband's inauguration. She remained in the Pierces' hotel room, writing letters of apology to her dead son. The usual inaugural balls and parties had been canceled out of respect for the family's mourning.

Jane Pierce and the Pierces' beloved son Benny.

Pierce was weakened by grief just at the time he needed all his strength. He had been nominated by a divided Democratic party more for his good looks and pleasing manner than for his accomplishments. He was naturally likable, with a boyish chin, a strong physique, and an amazing ability to remember the names of everyone he met. Even his critics liked him personally, but they also thought he was a political lightweight. He had been a congressman, a senator, and a wartime army officer, but he had no great record of accomplishment. Writer Ralph Waldo Emerson called Pierce a "nincompoop." A New York newspaper said that the new president "never made an effort in public life that can be recalled without an effort."

Yet this president was about to face some of the most difficult times in the country's history. Even though it was bursting with prosperity, the United States was being wrenched apart by ever-increasing debates about slavery. Extremists in the North, called abolitionists, wanted all slavery ended immediately. Extremists in the South insisted that slavery be permitted and protected not only in the South but in the many new territories now opening in the West. The Compromise of 1850, passed less than three years earlier, was intended to ease the fiery debates, but it had only made them worse. It would not be an easy time to be president. Pierce's longtime friend, Nathaniel Hawthorne, one of America's great authors, could see the gathering storm clouds. When Pierce won the presidential nomination, Hawthorne wrote, "Frank, I pity you—indeed I do, from the bottom of my heart."

The country needed a strong leader who could set a clear path and hold the nation together. Could Franklin Pierce become that leader?

Native of the Granite State ———————

Franklin Pierce was born November 23, 1804, in Hillsboro, New Hampshire, a state famous for its granite mountains. Franklin's father, Benjamin Pierce, had grown up in neighboring Massachusetts. In 1775, Benjamin was a 17-year-old farmhand plowing in his uncle's field when he heard that American patriots had fired on British troops at Lexington and Concord, Massachusetts, in the first battles of the American Revolution. Benjamin Pierce left the plow in the field, borrowed his uncle's musket, and hurried off to join the army. During the war, he rose to the rank of brigade major and fought alongside George Washington himself.

When the war was over, young Benjamin Pierce was commissioned to help survey a region in New Hampshire, to the north of Massachusetts. While there, he saw a promising piece of land near Hillsboro (then spelled Hillsborough) and bought it. He and a friend cleared the land, and he settled there. In 1787, he married Elizabeth Andrews. A year later Elizabeth gave birth to a daughter but died soon afterward. In 1790, Benjamin married Anna Kendrick, and they raised a large family. Franklin Pierce was born into a family that included his half-sister, two brothers, and two sisters. Two more children were born later.

The year Franklin was born, Benjamin Pierce moved his family from their log cabin to a much more spacious home that he built with his own hands. In the coming years, Franklin's father surrounded the house with gardens. Benjamin became an important leader and officeholder in the community and entertained many distinguished guests, including the famous Massachusetts senator Daniel Webster.

Benjamin Pierce had received very little education, and he was determined that his children would be more fortunate. When Franklin was eleven, he was enrolled in a private boarding school 14 miles (23 kilometers) from Hillsboro. Not long afterward, Franklin was so homesick that he sneaked away from the school and walked all the way home. The next day, his father drove Franklin halfway back to the school in a wagon and ordered the boy to walk the rest of the way.

In 1820, Franklin entered Bowdoin College at the age of 15. Located on the Atlantic seacoast in Brunswick, Maine, the school attracted accomplished young men from northern New England. Henry Wadsworth Longfellow, a year behind Pierce at Bowdoin, became one of America's most admired poets. Pierce

Franklin Pierce's boyhood home in Hillsboro, New Hampshire. The house is still standing, and today it holds memorabilia of Pierce's life and career.

met and befriended another young man in that class, Nathaniel Hawthorne, who later become one of America's most famous novelists. It was an odd pairing. Hawthorne was a shy, bookish boy, while Franklin was a confident and sociable youth. The two remained good friends for the rest of their lives.

Bowdoin College in Brunswick, Maine, as it looked when Franklin Pierce enrolled in 1820.

Nathaniel Hawthorne (1804–1864)

Born in Salem, Massachusetts, Nathaniel Hawthorne came from five generations of famed New Englanders. One of his ancestors was a judge in the Salem witchcraft trials, and his grandfather was a sea captain who fought so valiantly in the Revolutionary War that a ballad was written about him. Nathaniel's father was a merchant seaman who rose to the rank of captain and sailed to China, India, and Russia.

After graduating from Bowdoin, Hawthorne divided his time between writing and working at administrative jobs in the government. Franklin Pierce and other friends helped gain Hawthorne appointments to government positions.

Hawthorne struggled to create an American way of writing that would be different from British literature. In 1850, he published *The Scarlet Letter*, which has been called the first great American novel. The book tells the story of Hester Prynne, a single mother in a deeply religious New England town during the 1600s. Hester refuses to reveal the

Nathaniel Hawthorne and Franklin Pierce became friends in college. They remained friends for life, as Hawthorne became a distinguished author and Pierce became president.

identity of her baby's father and as punishment, she is forced to wear a scarlet letter *A* (standing for adultery) to remind people of her "crime."

In 1852, Hawthorne wrote the short biography of Franklin Pierce which was published during Pierce's campaign for president. After Pierce was elected, he appointed Hawthorne to be United States consul in Liverpool, England. Hawthorne died in 1864, during a trip with Pierce to New Hampshire's White Mountains.

During his first two years at college, Franklin spent more time enjoying a lively social life than he did studying. When grades were handed out, Franklin was last in his class. Embarrassed, Franklin resolved to change his habits and make up for lost time. When he graduated in 1824, he ranked fifth in his class. He also discovered a talent for public speaking. He had a strong voice and developed his skills as a speaker and debater.

After graduation, Pierce decided to study law. In those days a law student worked as a clerk to a practicing lawyer, helping in the office and studying in his spare time. Pierce worked in law offices in New Hampshire and in Massachusetts and was licensed to practice law in 1827.

During Pierce's boyhood, his father had served in a number of local offices. Now in 1827, Benjamin Pierce was elected governor of New Hampshire. Benjamin Pierce was a supporter of Andrew Jackson, who had lost a close presidential election in 1824. In 1828, both Benjamin and Franklin Pierce supported Jackson for president in New Hampshire. Jackson won election and was reelected in 1832.

In 1829, the year Andrew Jackson took office as president, Franklin Pierce was elected to the New Hampshire state legislature. At 24, he was its youngest member. He dazzled the chamber with what one friend called a "devilish fine" gift for making speeches. He was reelected three times, and in 1832 he

"Old Hickory"

During the War of 1812 between the United States and Great Britain, a tired group of American soldiers was marching from Natchez, Mississippi, to their homes in Tennessee. They had too little food and wondered if they would ever reach home. Then a tall gray-haired officer on foot pushed his way to the front of the group. He urged the men on and reassured them that they would all reach home alive. One soldier pointed to the officer—General Andrew Jackson—and yelled, "He's tough, tough as old hickory."

Jackson would prove his toughness many times, and the nickname stuck with him all the way to the White House. In 1815, he rallied a force at New Orleans to oppose an invading British army. The British were defeated with heavy casualties, and Jackson became a national hero.

As president, Jackson was like no president before him. Earlier presidents had been well-educated, wealthy gentlemen. Jackson was a rough-and-tumble man from a poor family who had made his reputation on the Tennessee frontier. His hot temper had gotten him into duels and gunfights, and he carried two bullets in his body as reminders. Yet he also knew how to lead men in battle and inspire voters.

He was elected as "the people's president," and pledged to take government out of the hands of the rich and influential. Until the 1820s, the right to vote in many states was restricted to white men who owned property and paid taxes. Jackson favored extending voting rights to all white male citizens. With his encouragement, many states revised their laws, allowing more and more white males to vote.

Jackson was a strong president with wide popular backing. He and his supporters established the modern Democratic party, and in 1832 he was the first president elected under its banner. Both Benjamin and Franklin Pierce soon joined the new party and remained in it for the rest of their lives.

☆ ★ ☆

General Andrew Jackson won a reputation as a military commander, served two terms as president, and helped establish the Democratic Party. Franklin Pierce and his father were devoted supporters of Jackson and his party.

was elected speaker (or leader) of the legislature, thanks to his talents and perhaps also to his father's influence. As speaker, he received $2.50 for each day the legislature was in session. Since it met only a few months a year, he continued his law practice.

By 1833, the Democratic party in New Hampshire was stronger than ever. Pierce was nominated to run for the U.S. House of Representatives and was elected. Not yet 30 years old, he was on his way to Washington, D.C.

Chapter 2

The City of Magnificent Distances ——

The newly elected young congressman from New Hampshire was eager to make a name for himself in Washington, D.C., in 1833. He was the son of a popular governor and had many friends in the Democratic party.

Washington was a much bigger city than any in New Hampshire, but Pierce may have been surprised at its emptiness. The capital had been established in 1799 in swampland along the Potomac River on the border between Virginia and Maryland. Although a grand plan was prepared, the new capital grew slowly and painfully. Then during the War of 1812, the city was captured by British troops, who burned the Capitol, the White House, and other public buildings. Rebuilding took years and set back the city's development. Still surrounded by swamps, the city often smelled bad, and residents were plagued by mosquitoes, some of which could transmit diseases.

British writer Charles Dickens visited Washington a few years later and called it "the city of magnificent distances." He described "spacious avenues that begin in nothing and lead nowhere; streets, miles long, that only want houses, roads, and inhabitants; public buildings that need but a public."

For Pierce, the city and the situation may have set him off balance. It was difficult to make progress in Congress, which was controlled by representatives who had served for many years. Freshman congressmen were expected to listen and learn, not to speak up. Like many congressmen, he lived in a boardinghouse while Congress was in session. Far from family and old friends, he stayed out late with other congressmen, eating and drinking in taverns. Soon he was better known as a drinking partner than as a talented congressman.

After his first session in Congress, Pierce went home to New Hampshire. There he proposed marriage to Jane Means Appleton, a shy, timid young woman he had been courting on and off for years. Jane's father had been president of Bowdoin College before Pierce enrolled. The Appleton family disapproved of Pierce. They were an aristocratic New England family who supported the Whig party and hated Andrew Jackson. They looked down their noses at the Pierces

A sketch of Washington about the time Franklin Pierce arrived to serve in Congress. It shows the Capitol in the distance and a long, broad avenue running up the hill. Cows still grazed in the fields near the Capitol.

from the backwoods of New Hampshire. Against this opposition, the couple was married in November 1834.

For the next session of Congress, Jane went with her new husband to Washington. From the beginning she disliked the city and the rough-talking politicians Franklin spent his evenings with. She especially hated the alcohol they drank in their late-night sessions. After that first visit, Jane often stayed in New Hampshire when Congress was in session. Franklin went to Washington alone and stayed in boardinghouses as before.

Jane's opposition to alcohol was no surprise. With many other men and women in New Hampshire, she was active in the temperance movement, a campaign to outlaw the sale and use of alcohol. Supporters of temperance argued that abusers of alcohol caused untold suffering, not only for those who drank it, but also for their families and children.

Pierce was reelected to the House in 1835. In 1837, the New Hampshire state legislature elected him to the U.S. Senate. At age 33, he was the youngest man in the chamber. There he met many of the giants of the American government. Daniel Webster, senator from Massachusetts, was an acquaintance of his father. John C. Calhoun of South Carolina was an eloquent spokesman for the southern states. Henry Clay of Kentucky was the "Great Compromiser," who had

A campaign sketch of Franklin Pierce shows his youthful good looks.

helped create the Missouri Compromise between slave and free states in 1820, when Franklin Pierce was just entering college.

In his four years as a congressman and six years as a senator, Pierce never stood out as one of the great men in Congress. He sponsored no important bills and made few memorable speeches. The only passion that Pierce revealed was a fierce opposition to *abolition*, a social and political movement that began in the northern states in the 1830s. Abolitionists called for the immediate end of slavery.

Pierce never favored slavery. His family had never owned slaves and Pierce personally thought the slave trade was evil. He did believe, however, that the slaveholding states were entitled to continue slavery, according to the U.S. Constitution. Like many political leaders of his day, he believed that agitation to end slavery threatened the existence of the United States, and he condemned the abolition movement as dangerous. With many others, Pierce believed that North and South should compromise on the future of slavery.

In 1842, Pierce announced that he was resigning from the Senate to return to New Hampshire and practice law. His wife Jane and their two young sons were at home in Concord. Jane had begged him to give up politics and spend more time at home. He may also have been discouraged by the growing power of antislavery forces in New England. Whatever the reasons, Franklin Pierce professed that he was coming home for good.

Abolition

In 1831, a Virginia slave named Nat Turner persuaded a small band of fellow slaves that they must revolt against their owner. On August 13, they killed the owner and his family. Other slaves joined the rebellion, and they killed nearly 60 white people. The white community mobilized and quickly overwhelmed the rebels. Turner was caught and hanged, along with other participants in the revolt. More than 200 slaves were lynched (killed without trial) by angry white mobs. The revolt caused a wave of fear in the slave states, and new laws were passed to control slaves.

In the North, however, those who believed slavery was a moral evil applauded Nat Turner's rebellion. Two years later, in 1833, the National Anti-Slavery Society was established. Its cause became known as abolition. The movement was especially strong in New England. By 1840, abolitionists were urging the government to end slavery. Southern leaders warned that if slavery was restricted, their states would withdraw from the United States to protect their rights to make their own policies on slavery.

When the United States gained nearly a million square miles of new territory in the 1840s, many in the North insisted that slavery must not spread to the new territories. Southerners insisted that slavery should be permitted. If a slave owner moved to a new territory, they asked, how could he be persuaded not to take his slaves? Moderates in the North and South were willing to consider some compromise, but the abolitionists refused to consider any compromise short of ending slavery.

☆ ☆ ☆

Home at Last

Back in New Hampshire, Franklin Pierce was a changed man. He gave up drinking and even helped direct a successful drive to ban liquor in his new hometown of Concord. He set up his law practice in Concord and soon met with great success.

After Franklin retired from the Senate, he and his family lived in Concord, New Hampshire, in the house above. Pierce's law offices were in the commercial building at the right.

Much of his practice involved the growing businesses in New Hampshire. As a former senator, he could help them lobby for fair treatment from the government. At the same time, he also practiced in the courtroom, where he seemed to regain his old speaking skills. He knew how to get a jury to see things from his side, appealing to both their reason and their emotions.

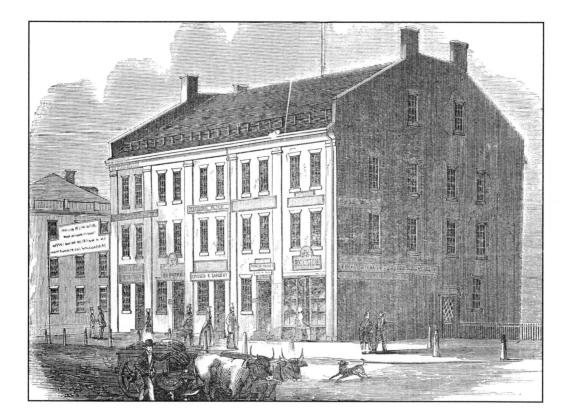

Pierce had promised Jane that he would never again run for office, but he did continue to work for the Democratic party in New Hampshire. In 1844, he helped organize the campaign for presidential candidate James K. Polk in the state. He was so successful that the grateful new president named Pierce a federal prosecutor. Later, Polk offered to appoint Pierce as attorney general of the United States, the country's top law-enforcement position. Pierce refused the offer. He had told Jane that they would not return to Washington, and he intended to keep his promise.

To Jane, these years in New Hampshire were the happiest times of her life. She seemed to overcome her *melancholy* (a condition doctors might call depression today). Still, the Pierces suffered a string of heartaches. Their first son, Franklin Pierce Jr., had died only three days after birth. Then in 1843, their four-year-old son Frank Robert died. Only Benjamin, then a year old, remained. Both Pierce and Jane were devoted to him.

War

The Pierces' happy home life was interrupted by the outbreak of the U.S.-Mexican War in 1846. The previous year, the United States had annexed Texas and made it a state. Mexico still claimed part of Texas. In 1846, U.S. and Mexican troops exchanged fire in the disputed territory, and the nations went to war.

While Pierce had turned down chances for election or appointment to high political positions, he could not resist the chance to fight for his country. His own father had fought in the American Revolution and had drilled local militia in Hillsboro when Franklin was a boy. Even though he was past 40 years old, Franklin Pierce enlisted.

Pierce had no previous military training, but his position as a former senator and a Democratic leader from New Hampshire brought him rapid promotion. By the time he sailed for Veracruz, Mexico, in 1847, he was a brigadier general and commanded a force of more than 2,500 soldiers.

Pierce's brigade was to join the army of General Winfield Scott, which had already captured Veracruz, on the shore of the Gulf of Mexico, and begun its long, hard march

Fast Facts

THE U.S.–MEXICAN WAR

Who: The United States and Mexico

When: The U.S. Congress declared war against Mexico on May 13, 1846. Fighting ended in September 1847. The Treaty of Guadalupe Hidalgo was signed on February 2, 1848.

Why: When the U.S. made Texas, a former territory of Mexico, a state in 1845, Mexico threatened war. U.S. troops entered territory claimed by both nations in 1846 and were attacked by Mexican forces in April 1846.

Where: The U.S. drove Mexican forces out of Texas and captured Monterrey in northern Mexico. They also captured parts of present-day New Mexico and California. In early 1847, a U.S. force landed at Veracruz, on Mexico's Gulf coast, and fought its way to Mexico City. The Mexican capital was occupied in September, ending the major fighting.

Outcome: In the Treaty of Guadalupe Hidalgo, Mexico ceded more than 500,000 square miles (1.3 million km^2) to the U.S., including all or most of present-day California, Nevada, Arizona, Utah, and New Mexico and parts of five other states. The U.S. paid Mexico $15 million and all claims of U.S. citizens against Mexico.

General Winfield Scott, commander of the U.S. army that battled its way from Veracruz, on the Gulf of Mexico, inland to Mexico City, the country's capital.

toward Mexico City. Scott was a legendary officer in the U.S. army. He was a huge man 6 feet (1.8 meters) tall and weighing 300 pounds (136 kilograms). He was a stickler for detail and insisted on strict military discipline, causing his troops to call him "Old Fuss and Feathers." Tropical heat and deadly tropical diseases were as challenging as the scrappy Mexican army which attacked them along the way.

General Pierce was eager to fight, but first he had to catch up with the rest of the army. In the brutal tropical heat, he led his troops on a march of 125 miles (200 km), defending against Mexican guerrilla fighters and doing his best to protect his men from tropical diseases. More than a month after arriving in Veracruz, Pierce's men joined the larger army, ready to fight as the armies approached the Mexican capital.

In August, Pierce led his men to their first major battle, at Contreras. On uneven, rocky terrain, they attacked the Mexican army head-on. Pierce and his men performed bravely, but before the battle was decided, Pierce's horse stumbled on the jagged rocks and lurched forward. Pierce flew forward and landed on the pommel of his saddle. Then the horse fell, landing on his leg and injuring his knee. Pierce briefly lost consciousness from the intense pain of his injuries. Within minutes, however, he was on his feet again and seeking a replacement for his injured horse. He stayed with his men through the battle and insisted on accompanying them as they pursued the Mexican army toward Mexico City.

General Pierce, on horseback, watches as his troops land in Mexico near Veracruz. They marched inland 125 miles to join General Scott's troops for the final battles of the war.

Although he performed well as a commander, Pierce did not escape the ridicule of some of his soldiers. Some may have resented fighting under a "political" general with little military experience. Behind his back, they retold the story of his injury and gave him the nickname "Fainting Frank."

This portrait of Pierce in his military uniform shows scenes of Mexico in the background.

In September, American forces captured Mexico City, and the Mexican army surrendered, ending the major fighting in the war. Pierce returned to New Hampshire, where he was welcomed as a hero. As he lifted Benny onto his shoulders and embraced Jane, Pierce accepted the congratulations of his friends and neighbors.

Chapter 3

Growth and Struggle ———————

On his return from Mexico in 1847, Pierce was New Hampshire's most famous son. He gained stature as a leader in the state, and his growing law practice brought him wealth.

The country was also experiencing a period of excitement and wealth. In a few short years, it had gained undisputed control of the vast territories west of the Rocky Mountains. President Polk had negotiated a treaty with Great Britain in 1846 that gave the United States full control of the Oregon country, including the present-day states of Oregon, Washington, and Idaho, and parts of Wyoming and Montana. Then in 1848, United States took possession of Mexico's northern territories, including California. That same year, gold was discovered in California, and soon thousands of Americans were rushing to the region hoping to strike it rich.

All this new territory brought a new crisis in the debate about slavery. Should slavery be permitted in the new territories or should it be prohibited? The House of Representatives, controlled by northern congressmen, passed a provision that no land received from Mexico should permit slavery. But the Senate, controlled by southern senators, refused even to bring the provision to a vote. The great debate over extending slavery would be the main topic of politics for years to come.

The Election of 1848

As the presidential election of 1848 approached, both the Democratic and Whig parties were divided between antislavery and proslavery factions. They each struggled to find a candidate who would appeal to both North and South in the hope of winning the election. After a bitter fight at their nominating convention, the Democrats nominated Lewis Cass of Michigan as their candidate. Cass, like Pierce, was seeking a compromise on slavery that would avoid the danger of breaking up the Union.

The Whigs nominated General Zachary Taylor, a hero of the early victories in the U.S.-Mexican War. Known to his troops as "Old Rough-and-Ready," Taylor was a career army officer who had never held an elective position or even voted in a presidential election. He had grown up in Kentucky and now owned large plantations in Louisiana and Mississippi and many slaves. Northern Whigs, fearful that Taylor would support slavery, insisted that the party nominate a northerner, Millard Fillmore of New York, for vice president.

It soon became clear that both parties planned to say as little as possible about slavery in the campaign, hoping to keep their northern and southern supporters together. This had an unexpected result. Some antislavery Whigs and Democrats were outraged that the burning issue of the day was being ignored by both parties. They walked out and established a new antislavery group, the Free-Soil party, at a huge convention in Buffalo, New York. Their main demand was that slavery be outlawed in the new territories. They nominated former Democratic president Martin Van Buren as their candidate.

The election was a close race between Cass and Taylor. The Free-Soil party had strong support only in a few northern states. In the end, however, Van Buren and the Free-Soilers had a big effect on the election. In New York, the state with the most people and the most electoral votes, Van Buren ran strongly, gaining most of his votes from former Democrats. Taylor and the Whigs won New York, and the state's electoral votes helped elect Zachary Taylor president.

President Zachary Taylor, who was elected in 1848.

The Struggle for Compromise ———————

Zachary Taylor proved to be a surprise to the South. He tried to arrange for California and New Mexico to enter the Union as nonslave states and seemed to believe that slavery should not spread to the new territories. Southerners in Congress angrily threatened that their states might *secede* from the Union—leave the United States.

At this point, the scene shifted to the U.S. Senate. There, Henry Clay of Kentucky, famous as the architect of other compromises between North and South in 1820 and 1833, proposed a plan. To please antislavery northerners, it proposed that California be admitted as a free state, and that the slave trade (but not slavery itself) be ended in Washington, D.C. To please proslavery southerners, it proposed a strong new law under which federal officials would help catch fugitive (or runaway) slaves in the North and return them to their owners in the South.

Debate on Clay's compromise went on for months. President Taylor refused to support it, preferring a plan of his own. Daniel Webster of Massachusetts, who opposed the extension of slavery, gave an eloquent address urging the Senate to support Clay's compromise in order to save the Union. Still, the Congress could not agree. Antislavery and proslavery groups condemned one part of the compromise and praised another, but refused to accept it all.

Henry Clay, who drafted the Compromise of 1850.

In July 1850, the debate was interrupted. President Taylor got sick on July 4, and five days later he died. Whigs and Democrats alike mourned the president, who had served for only 16 months. Vice President Millard Fillmore was sworn in to serve as president for the rest of Taylor's term.

Success and Disillusion ———————————————

The Compromise of 1850 seemed doomed to defeat. Its architect, Henry Clay, was elderly and ill, and left Washington to recover his health. Daniel Webster, a powerful supporter of the compromise, resigned from the Senate to serve as Fillmore's secretary of state. Then the proposal was saved by an unlikely pair— Whig president Millard Fillmore and Democratic senator Stephen Douglas of Illinois.

Both men agreed that the compromise was the best hope of ending the fiery disputes over slavery and assuring that the United States would remain whole and at peace. Douglas helped plan the strategy. He divided the compromise into five different bills. Then he worked feverishly to build support for each of the bills, one at a time. By September 1850, he succeeded in passing all five, and President Fillmore signed them into law. Supporters of the compromise held a celebration featuring the Marine band and a 100-gun salute.

Millard Fillmore, who became president in 1850 after the death of Zachary Taylor. Fillmore helped pass the Compromise of 1850, which Pierce strongly supported.

Although Franklin Pierce took no part in the debates in Washington, he strongly supported the Compromise of 1850. Like many Americans, he was weary of the debate on slavery and hoped that the compromise would put an end to the issue. Its provisions gave something to each side. It allowed a new state to choose against slavery, but it recognized the rights of slaveholders in the new Fugitive Slave Act.

Celebration over the compromise did not last long. Over the next two years, both North and South gradually came to hate it. Southerners realized that they had lost their control of the Senate by agreeing to admit California as a free state. After the first California election, there would be 32 senators from free states and only 30 from slave states. If more western lands became free states, they would elect more antislavery senators and congressmen. Before long, Congress might restrict or even end slavery altogether.

In the North, people were angered by the new Fugitive Slave Act, which made it a federal crime for any citizen (even in a northern state) to help a runaway slave. People were outraged that any African American, even one who had lived as a free person for many years, could be seized. Once seized, African Americans had no right to a trial and could not testify in their own defense. The federal commissioners who would decide fugitive slave cases were paid ten

Harriet Tubman, who helped 300 slaves reach freedom on the Underground Railroad.

dollars for every African American they returned to a slave owner and only five dollars for every one they released.

Mobs in northern cities stormed jails where African Americans were being held and rescued them, often helping them escape to Canada, beyond the reach of the hated law. Some states passed laws that required a trial before any former slave could be sent back to an owner in the South. Many individuals resolved to disobey the Fugitive Slave Act, risking fines and prison to help slaves travel through the North to freedom in Canada. Soon a secret network of escape routes crisscrossed the North. The network was called the Underground Railroad.

The Underground Railroad

The Underground Railroad had nothing to do with trains. The name comes from a kind of code that antislavery activists used when helping slaves escape their southern masters and reach freedom in Canada. Because helping runaway slaves was a crime, those who helped spoke of slaves as "passengers." Safe houses along the way, where the fugitives would be hidden and fed, were called "stations." Those who helped plan the fugitives' trips were called "conductors."

Passengers on the Underground Railroad traveled by night, usually on foot across fields and through forests, sometimes on horseback or by boat. They were told to look for a particular sign—a lantern or a window with a light—to recognize a station along the way.

The Underground Railroad began operation as early as the 1830s, but it grew quickly after the Fugitive Slave Act was passed in 1850. The number of passengers increased rapidly, and more and more northerners were willing to help. No one knows how many slaves found their way to freedom on the Underground Railroad—estimates run from 40,000 to more than 100,000. Only a small number of northern citizens actually sheltered escaping slaves or helped in other ways. Many others, however, resented the law and could be relied on not to report a fleeing slave.

Perhaps the most famous Railroad conductor was Harriet Tubman. She was an escaped slave who fled Maryland to freedom in the North. Tubman secretly returned to the South 19 times. Each time, she risked being captured and taken back into slavery. She helped 300 other slaves flee, including her own parents. She was such a beloved figure among slaves that they nicknamed her "Moses," because she led slaves to the promised land of freedom.

☆★☆

The Election of 1852

Even though the Fugitive Slave Act was unpopular in the North, Fillmore did all in his power to enforce it, even sending federal troops to areas where it was being ignored. As anger against the act increased, Fillmore's popularity decreased. By 1852, it was clear that he could not be elected to a full term as president. Both parties would need new candidates for president.

When the Democrats met in Baltimore, Maryland, two of the favorites for the presidential nomination were James Buchanan and Stephen Douglas. Buchanan had been a powerful senator from Pennsylvania, and later served as secretary of state. Douglas, the first-term senator from Illinois, had taken a leading role in passing the Compromise of 1850. Both Buchanan and Douglas were attractive candidates, but they had made many political enemies, too. Franklin Pierce helped pick New Hampshire's delegates to the nominating convention, but Pierce himself decided to stay home.

Deeply divided, delegates to the convention could not agree on a candidate for president. In 34 *ballots* (separate votes), no candidate came near the two-thirds majority needed to win the nomination. Finally, delegates began to look around for a "dark horse"—a fresh candidate who had not yet been considered. He should be good-looking and well spoken, and his views on issues—especially slavery—should be little known.

What Is a Dark Horse?

A "dark horse" is a surprise candidate and a political unknown, usually nominated when party members cannot choose between better-known politicians. The first dark horse president was James K. Polk, a Democrat who came out of obscurity to gain the Democratic presidential nomination in 1844 and be elected president. During the campaign, the opposing Whigs taunted him by chanting, "Who is James K. Polk?"

The term "dark horse" comes from racetrack slang. Owners of a talented racehorse sometimes dyed the horse a darker color and raced it under a different name. The owners bet on the "unknown" horse and made a handsome profit if it won. Racing fans knew that a dark horse with an unfamiliar name sometimes surprised bettors and won the race.

☆ ☆ ☆

On the 35th ballot, a New Hampshire delegate nominated Franklin Pierce from the floor. Since Pierce was not at the convention, he could not refuse the nomination. As the balloting continued, delegates realized that Pierce was a perfect compromise candidate. He was handsome and charming, he had fought bravely in the recent war. Best of all, he had been away from national politics for ten years, quietly practicing law. His views were not well known—and therefore could not offend anyone. On the 48th ballot, Pierce received the necessary two-thirds of the votes and became the Democratic candidate for president.

When Jane Pierce learned that Franklin Pierce had been nominated for president, she fainted. He had promised that he would never run for office again. Benny wrote to his mother, "I hope he won't be elected." Pierce may have been distressed at his family's reaction, but he decided to accept the nomination, even against their wishes.

Two weeks after the Democrats left Baltimore, the Whigs assembled there for their own convention. President Millard Fillmore put his name up, but the majority of Whig delegates voted for other candidates. The Whigs were as deeply divided as the Democrats. Their leaders also had too many political enemies to win the nomination. After dozens of ballots, they turned to a military hero, nominating General Winfield Scott, Franklin Pierce's commanding officer in Mexico, and the conqueror of Mexico City.

Pierce won the nomination by being an unknown, and Democrats wanted to keep him unknown. His advisers told him not to mention the divisive issue of slavery. Fortunately, presidential candidates at that time did little campaigning anyway, so Pierce had few chances to make mistakes. Reporters and voters visited Concord and chatted with Pierce on his front porch. They were impressed by his cheerful nature and his ability to remember their faces and names.

Democrats also emphasized Pierce's long connection to the party. The first president elected as a Democrat had been Andrew Jackson, whose nickname

A campaign banner for Franklin Pierce and his vice presidential running mate William R. King.

was "Old Hickory." The next Democratic president was James K. Polk, also from Tennessee, who ran as "Young Hickory." Pierce's campaign leaders called him "Young Hickory of the Granite Hills."

Pierce asked his old friend Nathaniel Hawthorne to write a campaign biography. Hawthorne had published his popular novel *The Scarlet Letter* only two years earlier, and was one of the most respected writers of the day. His biography described his friendship with Pierce beginning in college, and praised Pierce as a man and a political leader. Hawthorne included excerpts from Pierce's wartime diary, reminding readers about the candidate's military exploits.

Like the Democrats, the Whigs did their best to sidestep the real issues. Instead, they heaped insults and accusations on the opposing side. They dredged up rumors of Pierce's drinking exploits and compared the military record of "Fainting Frank" to the distinguished military career of General Scott. One newspaper called it the most "ludicrous, ridiculous, and uninteresting presidential campaign ever."

In the end, Scott doomed his own candidacy. Like Pierce, he was told to keep his slavery views to himself. Then one day when he was asked his views on the Fugitive Slave Act, Scott made the mistake of replying. He suggested that he did not completely approve of it and might want some changes in it. The

The Whig candidate for president, Winfield Scott, turned out to be a poor campaigner, helping Franklin Pierce win the election.

comment angered southern Whigs and destroyed Scott's chance to win southern states, which were essential to a Whig victory.

In the November election, Franklin Pierce won a strong victory, carrying even Winfield Scott's home state of Virginia. He won 254 electoral votes to Scott's 42. The popular vote was much closer—Pierce received about 1.6 million votes to Scott's 1.4 million.

At 48, Pierce was the youngest president up to that time. He looked forward to the challenge ahead in spite of his unhappy family and the deeply divided country.

Chapter 4

The President in Mourning ———————

The Pierce family prepared to move to Washington, D.C., where Franklin would take office in March 1853. This time, there would be no boardinghouses. They would live in the White House and Franklin Pierce would be president.

Then in January 1853, tragedy struck. Near North Andover, Massachusetts, the train the Pierces were riding home to New Hampshire ran off the tracks. Their car rolled down an embankment. Eleven-year-old Benny Pierce, the pride and joy of his parents, was killed instantly.

Benny's death left Jane Pierce shattered. She had given birth to three sons, and now all three had died in infancy or childhood. She came to believe that Benny's death was a punishment for her husband's election. Franklin Pierce was deeply touched by the boy's death and by his wife's suffering. When he arrived in Washington, he seemed like a different person, no longer the relaxed, smiling politician who had won the election. He seemed hesitant and unsure of himself. Jane Pierce did not appear in public at all.

Two other clouds shadowed Pierce's inauguration. Earlier in the year, Pierce helped arrange for Charles Atherton, a longtime friend and political supporter, to gain election as senator from New Hampshire. Atherton, born the same year as Pierce, had served in the New Hampshire legislature, the U.S. House, and the Senate. Pierce was counting on Atherton to be his eyes and ears in the Senate and to help pass the administration's measures. Soon after his election, however, Atherton died suddenly in New Hampshire, leaving Pierce without a strong ally in the Senate.

Pierce's vice president, William Rufus King, was also star-crossed. King had first been elected to Congress when Pierce was only seven years old. Before the 1852 election, King was a senator from Alabama. After the election, he became ill and traveled to Cuba to regain his health. In March, he was too sick to come to Washington for the inauguration. By special arrangement, he was sworn in as vice president in Havana. The next month he returned to his home in Alabama, where he died on April 18. Pierce served the rest of his term without a vice president.

On inauguration day, March 4, Pierce showed a spark of his great speaking skills, delivering his 20-minute speech from memory, without notes. As the youngest president to take office up to that time, he chose as his theme "Young

America," the title of a famous essay by New England philosopher Ralph Waldo Emerson. Like Emerson, Pierce saw "Young America" as a vital new nation that was throwing off the ideas of "Old Europe" and creating a new American civilization. He spoke confidently about further expansion of the country's territory and its growing importance in the world. He expressed support for the Compromise of 1850 and vowed that "no sectional or ambitious or fanatical

Franklin Pierce rides in procession down Pennsylvania Avenue in Washington on the day of his inauguration, March 4, 1853.

excitement" would arise over slavery. Pierce also confessed his grief caused by the tragedies that assailed him. "You have summoned me in my weakness," he said. "Now you must sustain me with your strength."

The Cabinet

For his cabinet, Pierce chose a cross section of Democratic party leaders, men who represented nearly every region of the country. Two of the appointments caused serious controversy. Pierce chose his old friend Jefferson Davis to serve as secretary of war. Few people doubted Davis's qualifications for the job. He was a graduate of the U.S. Military Academy and had served with distinction in the army. More recently, however, he had been a Democratic senator from Mississippi known for his strong pro-southern views. He had strongly opposed the Compromise of 1850 and had resigned from the Senate in protest when it passed.

The second controversial appointee was James Campbell of Pennsylvania, who was named postmaster general. Campbell was the first Roman Catholic to serve in a president's cabinet. His appointment led to anti-Catholic demonstrations, especially in areas where many Roman Catholic immigrants had recently arrived from Ireland. In fact, the appointment encouraged the growth of a new political party that demanded restrictions on the rights of immigrants and Catholics. This shadowy party soon gained a famous nickname—the "Know-Nothings."

The Know-Nothings

In 1845, a terrible famine struck Ireland, causing widespread poverty and starvation. In the next few years, hundreds of thousands emigrated to the United States. They took backbreaking jobs in the large cities and helped build new canals and railroads. The flood of immigrants led to a backlash, however. Workingmen complained that the Irish were taking jobs from native-born workers. Some political leaders and Protestant ministers warned that the new immigrants would try to put the government under the control of the Catholic Church. Franklin Pierce was opposed to anti-Catholic claims and was proud to appoint James Campbell to his cabinet.

Anti-immigrant and anti-Catholic politicians formed a shadowy group called the American party. It demanded that the government restrict immigration, require immigrants to live in the United States for 21 years before qualifying for citizenship (and voting rights), and make elective offices available only to people born in the United States. The group often worked secretly, supporting major-party candidates who agreed with their views. Party members were told not to reveal anything about the party's operations. If they were asked, they were told to say "I know nothing." Others outside the party began calling them "Know-Nothings" and the name stuck.

In 1854, Know-Nothings elected many of their own candidates and gained control of legislatures in Massachusetts and Delaware. In 1856, they nominated former president Millard Fillmore for president. He won 21 percent of the popular vote—more than one of every five votes cast. After 1856, as the country came ever closer to civil war, the Know-Nothing party lost its appeal, and it never played a large role in national politics again.

☆ ☆ ☆

In spite of controversy, the cabinet members Pierce chose were all approved by the Senate, and all of them remained in their jobs for the four years of his term. This was the only time before or since that a full cabinet served through a president's entire term of office.

The Gadsden Purchase

During his first year in office, Pierce was drawn into a deal that involved difficult relations with Mexico, the ambitions of railroad builders, and the competition between the North and the South.

The Treaty of Guadalupe Hidalgo, which ended the U.S.-Mexican War in 1848, had left boundaries between Mexico and the New Mexico Territory of the United States vague through the deserts of the Southwest. The disputed land lay south of the Gila River. Residents of New Mexico threatened to occupy the region, and Mexico pledged to defend it.

In the United States, southern railroad owners had a special interest in the disputed territory. Surveys suggested that it would provide the most practical route for a new transcontinental railroad running through Texas and on to southern California. Encouraged by Secretary of War Jefferson Davis, Pierce named James Gadsden, president of a southern railroad, as minister to Mexico. Gadsden was authorized to negotiate purchase of the territory from Mexico's president

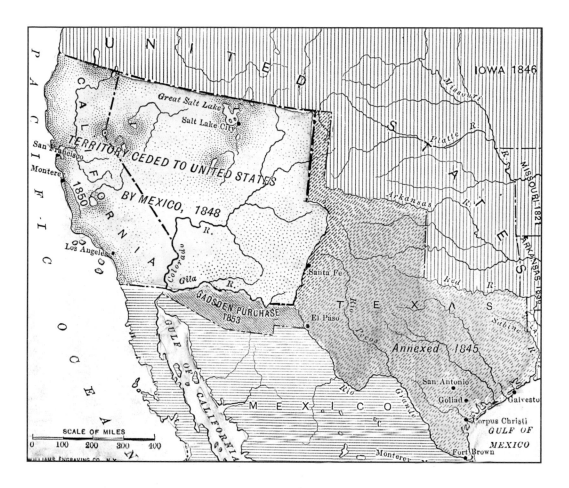

This map shows the Gadsden Purchase, a slice of land stretching from El Paso, Texas, to the Colorado River.

Antonio López de Santa Anna. Gadsden returned with an agreement for purchase of a large tract of land south of the Gila for $15 million.

The Gadsden Purchase ran into trouble when presented to the Senate for approval. Northern senators saw it as a giveaway to proslavery forces in the

South. They strongly favored a northern route for the transcontinental railroad. Senator Stephen Douglas of Illinois was especially concerned. He and his railroad friends were planning a line to start in Chicago (Douglas's home) and cross the Rocky Mountains to Sacramento, California. The Senate rejected Gadsden's first purchase agreement.

Building new railroads required advances in engineering to build long bridges across rivers. This bridge was on the Baltimore and Ohio Railroad.

The Transcontinental Railroad

By the 1850s, railroads were becoming the most important means of travel and shipping. Ambitious business-men formed companies to plan and build new routes that could bring farm goods to market and carry travelers safely and quickly. They often received grants of land and other advantages from local and state governments.

Now that the United States stretched from the Atlantic Ocean to the Pacific, railroads were sure to become more important. A transcontinental railroad would be needed to connect the East to California and Oregon. Since the federal government owned most of the land between the Mississippi River and the Pacific, railroad builders began asking for land grants and other assistance.

A big question remained—which was the best route across the country? Southerners favored a route that would run through Texas to southern California. It would be cheaper to build, they argued, since the mountains were not nearly as high in the south. Northerners wanted a northern route which would pass through promising agricultural land in the Great Plains. It would end in northern California, where most of the state's people then lived.

Pierce tried to encourage both northern and southern railroad planners, and the dispute on the best route continued for years afterward. Finally, in 1862, after the southern states left the Union and were at war with the North, Congress chose a northern route, and work began. On May 10, 1869, the line was completed. Later, other transcontinental routes would be built, including one that crossed the Gadsden Purchase.

☆ ☆ ☆

Douglas stood firm. If the president wanted the Gadsden Purchase passed, he would have to agree to help the northern rail builders, too. Douglas had a plan that would help northern railroads. If the president would support his plan, Douglas would support the purchase from Mexico. Douglas's plan would create a firestorm in the country and contribute to the downfall of Pierce, Douglas, and the Democratic party.

The Slavery Debate Continues ──────────

Franklin Pierce wished fondly that the country could put the debates on slavery behind it and concentrate on other matters. The debates continued to grow more heated, however, and it seemed that every other issue he took up soon involved the rivalry and hatred between North and South.

In the North, the abolitionist movement continued to grow more and more powerful. Through almanacs and magazines, they painted horrifying pictures of slave life, often using "testimonials" from slaves themselves. The movement gained many new converts after the Fugitive Slave Act was passed in 1850. Then in 1852, the year Pierce was elected, a quiet woman named Harriet Beecher Stowe wrote a novel called *Uncle Tom's Cabin*, telling the story of a group of slaves, including the old slave Uncle Tom, a deeply Christian man, who is sold to an evil slave-master named Simon Legree and is finally killed. The book sold

Uncle Tom's Cabin

Harriet Beecher Stowe was the daughter of a famous New England religious leader and preacher. From 1832 to 1850, she lived with her family in Cincinnati, Ohio, where she gained a deep sympathy for the slaves who lived just across the Ohio River in the slave state of Kentucky. Shortly after moving back to New England in 1850, she wrote *Uncle Tom's Cabin*.

In the book, Stowe portrays the heartbreak when a slave family is separated and sold to different owners. She shows the heart-stopping fear slaves felt when escaping from their masters to gain freedom in the North. In Uncle Tom himself, she shows a God-fearing slave horribly mistreated by a cruel white master.

The melodramatic story brought the evils of slavery to life for thousands of Americans. According to legend, when President Abraham Lincoln met Harriet Beecher Stowe during the Civil War, he said, "So you're the little woman who wrote the book that started this Great War!"

★ ★ ☆

more than 300,000 copies in its first year, and moved many readers to hate slavery. In the South, the book was condemned and ridiculed, and copies of it were burned rather than read. *Uncle Tom's Cabin* was not a book about politics, but it helped change the political world by hardening positions on both sides.

Defenders of slavery also wrote melodramatic stories in which wise plantation owners protected and cared for their slaves through difficult times. They portrayed slaves as innocent and childlike, not able to care for themselves or make wise decisions. They played to the widespread belief that African Americans were not as intelligent or able as white Americans. Long after slavery was abolished, this view of African Americans appeared often in minstrel shows and other popular entertainments.

Altogether, the country was dividing into two camps—for slavery and against slavery. Franklin Pierce and other political leaders seemed unable to stop this process, and they could see that there was less and less middle ground on which to build a compromise.

Chapter 5

The Kansas-Nebraska Act ──────────

In early 1854, Pierce was still urging Congress to pass the Gadsden Purchase when Stephen Douglas came to him with a proposal. Douglas supported a northern route for the transcontinental railroad. Pierce wanted the Gadsden Purchase to help southern railroad interests. Douglas wanted help for supporters of a northern route. He wanted to divide the huge Nebraska Territory in two—Kansas and Nebraska—and to encourage the territories to apply for statehood. He believed statehood would help the railroad builders gain land and remove American Indians, who still lived in the region. However, statehood would raise the issue of slavery once again.

Douglas proposed that the new act provide for residents of the new territories to decide the slavery issue for themselves by voting on it. This procedure received the impressive-sounding name *popular*

A portrait of President Franklin Pierce.

sovereignty. Douglas seemed to think that Kansas, bordering the slave state of Missouri, would likely decide in favor of slavery, while Nebraska would decide against it.

Pierce understood immediately that Douglas's plan would cause an uproar. In 1820, 34 years earlier, the Missouri Compromise had provided that the territory occupied by both Kansas and Nebraska be free of slavery. Many northern congressmen would refuse to vote for any act that changed that provision. Douglas also knew that the proposal was risky, but he pointed out that slave states were already outnumbered by free states. He raised the possibility that if both Kansas and Nebraska became free states, southern states might secede, breaking the country in two.

Douglas also had another argument. Pierce was eager for the Senate to pass the Gadsden Purchase and to approve his appointments to high government jobs. If Pierce would support Douglas's Kansas-Nebraska bill, Douglas could help Pierce get his wishes. Pierce admired and feared Douglas for the power he exercised in the Senate. Finally, he agreed to support Douglas's Kansas-Nebraska Act.

When Douglas's Kansas-Nebraska plan was made public, it caused a firestorm throughout the North. People who wanted to keep slavery from spreading—abolitionists and moderates alike—joined to oppose the act. Whigs

Senator Stephen Douglas of Illinois, the architect of the Kansas-Nebraska Act. Known as the "Little Giant," Douglas was a powerful force in the Democratic party.

were so split on the issue that the party broke in half, southerners voting for the act and northerners voting against it. The division was almost as severe in the Democratic party.

Douglas had counted his votes, however. With the support of southern Democrats and Whigs and a few northerners determined to preserve the Union, the Kansas-Nebraska Act passed. President Pierce signed it into law on May 30, 1854. True to his word, Douglas also worked to pass the Gadsden Purchase and President Pierce's appointments.

Even before Congress passed the Kansas-Nebraska Act, some northern Whigs and Democrats began to leave their parties to organize a new political party to oppose the spread of slavery. It would be called the Republican party. Within two years, it would replace the Whigs as the second major party in the United States. As the elections of 1854 approached, Republicans were joined by Know-Nothings and other opponents of the Democratic party.

Stephen Douglas

A short man with broad shoulders, a striking face, and an extraordinary speaking style, Stephen Douglas gained the nickname the "Little Giant." He dearly wanted to be president someday. In the end, he may have been too clever to achieve his greatest ambition. His Kansas-Nebraska Act was so unpopular that the Democratic party refused to nominate him—or Franklin Pierce—for president in 1856.

In 1858, Douglas ran for reelection to the Senate in Illinois against a rising Republican lawyer, Abraham Lincoln. In a series of debates, Lincoln and Douglas debated the issues surrounding slavery. Douglas argued that the South must be kept in the Union even if it meant allowing slavery in the territories. Lincoln opposed the spread of slavery no matter what the South might do. Lincoln's supporters believed that he won the debates, but Douglas was reelected to the Senate.

In 1860, Douglas was finally nominated by the Democrats for the presidency, but it was too late. Southern Democrats refused to support him and nominated their own candidate. With the party fatally divided, Douglas lost to the Republican candidate—Abraham Lincoln. Soon afterward, southern states began to secede from the Union and the Civil War began. Douglas declared his support for President Lincoln and urged "every American to rally around the flag of his country." Only two months later, Douglas died of a fever at the age of 48.

☆ ☆ ☆

In 1858, Douglas and Abraham Lincoln ran against each other for the Senate in Illinois. One of their seven famous debates took place at Knox College in Galesburg. The debates, about issues relating to slavery, were published in newspapers throughout the country. They made Lincoln a national figure in the Republican party, but Douglas was reelected to the Senate.

Through the summer and fall, Democrats could see their support melting away as the Kansas-Nebraska Act was condemned throughout the North. In November, election results confirmed the country's anger. Democrats lost their majority in the House of Representatives, and hundreds of local candidates were defeated. This huge shift would cripple the Pierce administration through its last two years in office.

"Bleeding Kansas"

In the meantime, conditions in Kansas went from bad to worse. Opponents of slavery in New England organized to send new antislavery settlers to the territory who would vote against a proslavery constitution. In the South, supporters of slavery sent proslavery settlers. They also enlisted residents of Missouri to cross the line into Kansas to vote in the constitutional election. No one knew just how many residents Kansas had, so nearly anyone could vote.

In the first vote on a constitution, free-state voters refused to participate, believing the election was rigged. Proslavery forces won a big victory. In a second election, more than 6,000 people voted, even though the territory had only 2,900 registered voters. Proslavery forces won again and began setting up a government that would punish any person who spoke publicly against slavery. Free-staters established their own capital and wrote their own constitution. Pierce

The States During the Presidency of Franklin Pierce

ORIGINAL STATES

recognized the proslavery government and ordered the free-state government to disband.

As two governments battled for control of the territory, violence took the place of persuasion. People on both sides were threatened, barns were burned, homes were ransacked. The Kansas residents who simply wanted to settle down and farm were caught in the middle. In early 1856, a congressional committee visited Kansas and concluded that the constitutional votes had been fraudulent and recommended that the free-state government be recognized. President Pierce ignored the advice.

Then on May 21, 1856, a supposed posse of the proslavery government visited Lawrence, Kansas, a free-state center. During the day, they burned the Free State Hotel to the ground, destroyed the printing presses of two antislavery newspapers, and terrorized the citizens. Only days later, the radical abolitionist John Brown and a small group of men attacked five proslavery men in Pottawatomie Creek and hacked them to death with swords. One newspaper called the ugly situation "Bleeding Kansas." It put the blame on Franklin Pierce and Stephen Douglas.

The violence spread even to Congress. Two days after Senator Charles Sumner of Massachusetts delivered a blistering speech called "The Crime Against Kansas," Congressman Preston Brooks of South Carolina attacked

In May 1856, a posse from Kansas's proslavery government burned down the Free State Hotel in Lawrence (above) and destroyed printing presses used by antislavery newspapers. Days later, radical abolitionist John Brown (right) raided Pottawatomie, Kansas, brutally murdering five proslavery citizens.

Sumner. Before anyone could stop him, Brooks beat Sumner unconscious with a cane. The Massachusetts senator was so badly injured that he did not return to the Senate floor for nearly three years.

Many called on Pierce to send federal troops to restore order in Kansas, but he resisted. In the summer of 1856, however, he sent a new federal governor, John W. Geary, who began to bring back law and order. Still, the conflict would continue even after Pierce left office. Kansans finally agreed on a free-state constitution in 1859 and the state was admitted to the Union in 1861, after the southern states had seceded from the Union.

As his term entered its last months, Pierce found himself deeply despised in his own region of the country. A New Hampshire judge accused him of having "the damndest black heart that was ever placed in a mortal bosom." A Whig senator from Maine wrote, "Pierce is a runt miserable dog, and seems bent on destroying his country, as well as himself."

The Opening of Japan ────────────────

One bright spot for the Pierce administration concerned events on the other side of the world. Pierce believed it was the destiny of the United States to expand its influence in the world. Even as the issues of slavery at home took more and more of his attention, Pierce and his administration pursued an aggressive foreign policy.

In 1852, after Pierce had been elected but before he took office, an expedition commanded by Commodore Matthew Perry set sail for Japan. President Millard Fillmore had ordered Perry to deliver a message from the American president to the emperor of Japan requesting Japan to open commercial relations with the United States. For 200 years, Japan had forbidden its people to leave the country and refused permission to foreigners to visit or trade.

On July 8, 1853, Perry sailed into Edo Bay, near present-day Tokyo. The Japanese were astounded by Perry's steamships, which were puffing huge clouds of black smoke. They had never seen a steamship before and believed at first that the ships were on fire, or perhaps that they were volcanoes. Perry came ashore dressed in a showy uniform and accompanied by an armed escort. He demanded an audience with the emperor. Although he delivered President Fillmore's letter, the Japanese refused to enter negotiations. Perry and his ships left Japan and sailed to China, where they awaited instructions from the Pierce administration.

In February 1854, Perry returned to Japan, this time with seven armed ships to impress and frighten the Japanese. When he came ashore in March, he was preceded by a military band playing "The Star-Spangled Banner." He also brought examples of recent inventions to amaze and impress the Japanese, including a scale model of a steam locomotive and a camera. One of his other

Commodore Matthew Perry prepares to meet the Japanese commissioners during his visit. His sailors, with guns and bayonets, stand at attention at the left.

exhibits was an illustrated book with colored engravings showing U.S. ships firing long-range guns at the Mexican city of Veracruz. The threat was clear—U.S. ships could fire guns at Japanese cities if it wished.

After weeks of negotiation, the Japanese reluctantly signed the Treaty of Kanagawa, agreeing to care for any shipwrecked American sailors, to set up a station to sell coal to passing U.S. steamships, and to give the United States the right to send diplomats to the court of Japan. Perry's "gunboat diplomacy" marked the beginning of huge changes for Japan. Soon other world trading powers were seeking trading rights there, and gradually, Japan opened its ports to world trade. In 1856, Pierce's secretary of state, William Marcy, sent another mission to Japan which succeeded in negotiating further concessions.

The Campaign to Buy Cuba ———————

Pierce's other adventure in foreign policy did not end as well. By 1853, southerners were urging the U.S. government to buy Cuba from Spain. That island, only 90 miles (145 km) from Florida, would extend the territory of the United States into the Caribbean region. Since it had a plantation economy, Cuba seemed a perfect place for the extension of slavery. If Cuba became a state, it could help balance the votes of new free states in the western territories.

Pierce seemed eager to pursue the idea. Cubans seemed ready to revolt against Spain, and Spain itself was deeply in debt to other European nations. In addition, American merchants had many grievances against Spanish officials in Cuba. Pierce appointed Pierre Soulé as U.S. minister to Spain, with instructions to offer money to buy Cuba. Soulé was a native of France and an influential lawyer in New Orleans. He was widely known for his strong support for adding Cuba to the United States—either by purchase or by military action.

At the Spanish court, Soulé soon offended the queen and outraged government leaders. He met with Spaniards who wanted to overthrow the Spanish government. Even though Soulé could offer as much as $130 million to buy Cuba, the angry Spaniards were in no mood to discuss the sale of their colony.

In 1854, Secretary of State Marcy ordered Soulé to meet with the U.S. ministers to Great Britain and France, James Buchanan and John Mason, to agree on a course of action. The men met first at Ostend (in present-day Belgium) and later in Aix-la-Chapelle (now in Germany). They wrote a document called the Ostend Manifesto, outlining their recommendations. The United States should make every effort to buy Cuba, they said, outlining all the advantages for both countries. Then the document ended with a threat—if Spain refused to sell Cuba, it said, the United States might find it necessary to take possession of the island by force.

Pierce and Secretary of State Marcy both personally agreed with the manifesto. However, it reached them just as the Democrats were suffering disastrous losses in the elections of 1854. When parts of the manifesto began appearing in newspapers, there was a firestorm of criticism in the northern states. Political leaders condemned it as another plot by supporters of slavery in the South. Pierce and Marcy were forced to reject the Ostend Manifesto and to give up further efforts to gain possession of Cuba. Pierre Soulé soon resigned as minister to Spain and returned to Louisiana.

This was the last major effort of the Pierce administration to add territory to the United States. Weakened by the losses in the 1854 elections and distracted by the continuing violence in Kansas, the administration pursued no further adventures overseas.

Life in the White House

As a large part of the country turned away from Franklin Pierce, the White House remained a joyless place. Jane Picrce continued to mourn the death of her son and rarely appeared at public events. Her aunt, Abigail Kent Means, served as the White House hostess, and at times Varina Davis, wife of Jefferson Davis, assisted. When Jane Pierce did appear, she was described as having "a woebegone face . . . sunken eyes, skin like ivory."

Jane Pierce, the ghostly first lady in the White House, who rarely appeared in public during her husband's presidency.

Left to carry out his duties without much support from his wife, and deserted by many of his old political friends and supporters, Franklin Pierce was a lonely president in a White House one visitor called "cold and cheerless." Some reports suggest that he eased his unhappiness by drinking alone.

The Election of 1856

Pierce's reputation continued to decline during 1856, as mobs in Kansas looted and killed and he seemed powerless to end the violence. Still, he had not lost his taste for the presidency. He let Democratic party leaders know that he wanted to be a candidate for reelection in November.

At the nominating convention, it became clear that he had little chance for the nomination. Democrats saw clearly that the man whose name was connected to "Bleeding Kansas" and to a plot to acquire Cuba would stand little chance of being reelected. The convention settled instead on James Buchanan, long a powerful senator from Pennsylvania, who had served as Pierce's minister to Great Britain. Buchanan was elected president, defeating Republican John C. Frémont

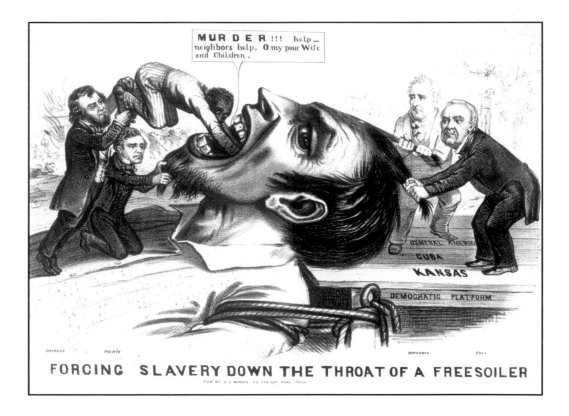

A Republican cartoon during the presidential campaign in 1856 shows Stephen Douglas and Franklin Pierce (left) "forcing slavery down the throat of a Freesoiler [Republican]." The Democrats' presidential candidate, James Buchanan, is at the right, holding the Free-Soiler down by his hair.

and American Party (Know-Nothing) candidate Millard Fillmore. The Whig party, which split over the Kansas-Nebraska Act, did not run a candidate.

Franklin and Jane Pierce left the White House quietly even before Pierce's term was over. Jane was so ill that she had to be carried to a waiting carriage. Pierce, who had been elected with great hopes of bringing peace and agreement to the country, was leaving office with few friends and few accomplishments.

Retirement

The Pierces returned to New Hampshire after leaving the White House. Soon afterward, however, they sailed to the Caribbean, where they hoped the climate would improve Jane Pierce's health. She had been diagnosed with tuberculosis, a slow wasting disease that was then often fatal. From there, they sailed to Europe, still in search of a healthful climate.

Meanwhile, James Buchanan was struggling unsuccessfully with divisions and growing violence in the United States. Fighting continued in Kansas. In Congress, the House was controlled by the North and the Senate by the South. In 1859, radical abolitionist John Brown attacked a federal arsenal in Harpers Ferry, Virginia (now West Virginia), seeking arms and ammunition for an uprising against slavery. Brown and his small band were captured and Brown was executed, but the incident further separated North and South.

The Pierces returned to New Hampshire in 1860 and settled in Concord. That year, the Democrats nominated Senator Stephen Douglas for president, but by now, even the Democratic party could not hold together. Even though Douglas was sympathetic to southern claims, southern Democrats walked out of the nominating convention and chose their own candidate, John C. Breckinridge. With the Democratic vote split between two candidates, Republican Abraham Lincoln was elected. Soon after the election, southern states prepared to secede from the Union. President Buchanan stood by as southern states took control of federal arsenals, and war approached.

Franklin Pierce hoped until the very last that a compromise might avoid the civil war he had worked so hard to prevent. It was no use. Only weeks after Lincoln took office in 1861, the first shots were fired at Fort Sumter, in the harbor of Charleston, South Carolina. The South organized as the Confederate States of America and chose as its president Pierce's old friend and secretary of war, Jefferson Davis. "Civil war has only horror for me," Davis wrote to Pierce before the fighting began, "but whatever circumstances demand shall be met as a duty and I trust to be so discharged that you will not be ashamed of our former connection or cease to be my friend."

Pierce supported the Union during the war, but he openly criticized the actions of President Lincoln. Many of his neighbors, devoted to the northern

During the Civil War, Jefferson Davis, Pierce's friend and secretary of war, was elected president of the Confederate States of America, the new government of the southern states.

cause, refused to speak to him. In 1863, Union armies won major victories at Gettysburg and Vicksburg, and the tide began to turn against the South. Late that year, Jane Pierce lost her long battle with tuberculosis. She died at the home of her sister in Andover, Massachusetts, and was buried in the Pierce family plot in Concord, New Hampshire.

In April 1865, the Confederate Army of Northern Virginia surrendered to Union forces, ending the major fighting. Only days later, President Lincoln was killed by an assassin in Washington. That night, a threatening mob gathered around Franklin Pierce's home in Concord. His neighbors remembered him for extending slavery into the Kansas territory, and they had heard false rumors that he was a member of a secret pro-southern society. Pierce appeared, expressed his sorrow for the assassination, and persuaded the crowd to break up and go home.

Four years later, in 1869, Pierce became ill and died on October 8, a few weeks short of his 65th birthday. His addiction to alcohol may have contributed to his death.

Legacy

Franklin Pierce seemed to have many of the qualities and talents of a successful president. He was handsome, well spoken, and intelligent. He had shown his

Franklin Pierce in retirement.

skills as a politician in New Hampshire and in Congress. Perhaps if he had been president during a more peaceful time, he would have contributed more.

Pierce was unlucky in many ways. His party chose him not because of his principles or his great service to the country, but because his views and actions were little known and he had few enemies. He entered office soon after a terrible family tragedy—the death of his young son—and the long illness of his wife made his personal life lonely.

Worst of all, Pierce was president during one of the most troubled times in the country's history. Pierce devoted his efforts to finding a compromise between North and South. Yet the compromises he supported seemed to make both sides more angry, and he received hate mail and threats from both North and South. He gradually understood that the division between the regions was so great that there was less and less chance to bring the two sides together. Perhaps a very strong president might have succeeded, but Pierce was not strong. It often seemed that he preferred to follow the lead of stronger men such as Jefferson Davis and Stephen Douglas.

Pierce's reputation as president was also damaged because the people he thought were the greatest threat to the country—those who wanted to abolish slavery—gained their objective in the Civil War. After the war, most historians saw his presidency from the abolitionists' point of view. Pierce became a villain because he supported compromises that would continue the evils of slavery. Even if he had been a stronger and more effective president, later historians would have put him on the "wrong" side of the story.

Franklin Pierce

Birth:	November 23, 1804
Birthplace:	Hillsborough, New Hampshire
Parents:	Benjamin and Anna Kendrick Pierce
Brothers & Sisters:	Benjamin Kendrick (1790–1850)
	Nancy (1792–1837)
	John Sullivan (1796–1824)
	Harriet B. (1800–?)
	Charles Grandison (1803–1828)
	Charlotte (?–?)
	Henry Dearborn (1812–1880)
Education:	Graduated from Bowdoin College, 1824
Occupation:	Lawyer
Marriage:	To Jane Means Appleton, November 10, 1834
Children:	(see First Lady Fast Facts, next page)
Political Party:	Democratic
Public Offices:	1829–1833 New Hampshire House of Representatives
	1833–1836 U.S. House of Representatives
	1836–1842 United States Senate
	1847 Brigadier General, U.S.-Mexican War
	1853–1857 14th President of the United States
His Vice President:	William Rufus King (1786–1853), died in office
Major Actions as President:	1853 Authorized Gadsden Purchase, acquiring southern Arizona and New Mexico from Mexico
	1854 Signed the Kansas-Nebraska Act
	1854 Supported Treaty of Kanagawa, opening Japanese trade with the United States
Death:	October 8, 1869, in Concord, New Hampshire
Age at Death:	64 years
Burial Place:	Old North Cemetery in Concord, New Hampshire

Fast Facts Jane Means Appleton Pierce

Birth:	March 12, 1806
Birthplace:	Hampton, New Hampshire
Parents:	Jesse and Elizabeth Means Appleton
Brothers & Sisters:	Mary, Frances, Robert, others unknown
Education:	Taught at home
Marriage:	To Franklin Pierce, November 10, 1834
Children:	Franklin Jr. (1836–1836)
	Frank Robert (1839–1843)
	Benjamin (1841–1853)
Death:	December 2, 1863, in Concord, New Hampshire
Age at Death:	57 years
Burial Place:	Old North Cemetery in Concord, New Hampshire

Timeline

1804	1806	1824	1827	1829
Franklin Pierce is born on November 23 in Hillsborough, New Hampshire.	Jane Means Appleton is born in Hampton, N.H.	Pierce graduates from Bowdoin College.	Pierce is licensed to practice law. His father Benjamin is elected governor of New Hampshire.	Pierce elected to New Hampshire House of Representatives; serves four years.

1846	1847	1848	1850	1852
U.S. declares war on Mexico; Pierce enlists to fight.	Pierce is injured at Battle of Contreras; returns home by year's end.	Treaty of Guadalupe Hidalgo ends U.S.-Mexican War.	Compromise of 1850 is passed; it includes a new Fugitive Slave Act.	Pierce is elected 14th president of the United States. Harriet Beecher Stowe publishes *Uncle Tom's Cabin*.

1857	1858	1860	1861	1863
Pierce leaves office, travels with wife to the Caribbean and Europe.	Senatorial candidates Abraham Lincoln and Stephen Douglas debate over slavery.	Franklin and Jane Pierce return to New Hampshire. Republican Abraham Lincoln is elected president; first southern states secede.	The Civil War begins.	Jane Pierce dies at 57. President Lincoln issues Emancipation Proclamation, freeing slaves in the South.

FORCING SLAVERY DOWN THE THROAT OF A FREESOILER

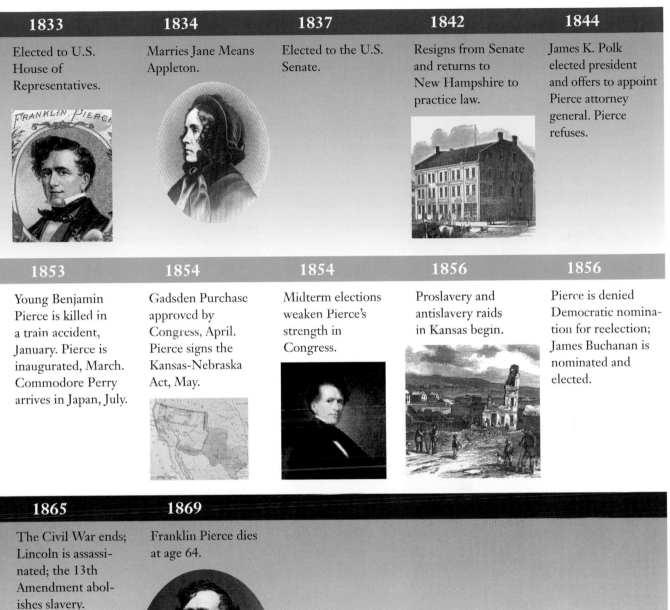

1833
Elected to U.S. House of Representatives.

1834
Marries Jane Means Appleton.

1837
Elected to the U.S. Senate.

1842
Resigns from Senate and returns to New Hampshire to practice law.

1844
James K. Polk elected president and offers to appoint Pierce attorney general. Pierce refuses.

1853
Young Benjamin Pierce is killed in a train accident, January. Pierce is inaugurated, March. Commodore Perry arrives in Japan, July.

1854
Gadsden Purchase approved by Congress, April. Pierce signs the Kansas-Nebraska Act, May.

1854
Midterm elections weaken Pierce's strength in Congress.

1856
Proslavery and antislavery raids in Kansas begin.

1856
Pierce is denied Democratic nomination for reelection; James Buchanan is nominated and elected.

1865
The Civil War ends; Lincoln is assassinated; the 13th Amendment abolishes slavery.

1869
Franklin Pierce dies at age 64.

Glossary

abolition: a social and political movement that began in the northern states in the 1830s, campaigning for the immediate end, or abolition, of slavery

ballot: a vote to choose candidates for office at political convention; if no candidate receives the required vote, new ballots are taken until a candidate wins

melancholy: a condition of deep sadness and despair that modern physicians might call depression

popular sovereignty: in the mid-1800s, a belief that residents of a new territory or state should determine by vote whether to permit or prohibit slavery

secede: in the mid-1800s, the action of a state to leave the United States (the Union) and renounce the powers of the central (federal) government

Further Reading

Ferry, Steven. *Franklin Pierce: Our Fourteenth President*. Chanhassen, MN: Child's World, 2001.

Somervill, Barbara A. *Franklin Pierce*. Minneapolis, MN: Compass Point Books, 2002.

Welsbacher, Anne. *Franklin Pierce*. Edina, MN: Checkerboard Library, 2002.

Young, Jeff C. *Franklin Pierce*. Berkeley Heights, NJ: Enslow Publishers, 2002.

MORE ADVANCED READING

Gara, Larry. *The Presidency of Franklin Pierce*. Lawrence: University Press of Kansas, 1991.

Nichols, Roy F. *Franklin Pierce: Young Hickory of the Granite Hills*. Newtown, CT: American Political Biography Press, 1993.

Places to Visit

★ ★ ★ ★ ★

The Pierce Manse

14 Penacook Street
P.O. Box 425
Concord, NH 03302
(603) 225-2068

The home of the Pierce family from 1842 to 1848, when Pierce was practicing law in Concord before being elected president.

The Pierce Homestead

P.O. Box 896
Hillsborough, NH 03244
(603) 478-3165
http://www.franklinpierce.ws/homestead/
contents.html

The boyhood home of Franklin Pierce. It was built by his father Benjamin and completed about the time Franklin was born.

The White House

1600 Pennsylvania Avenue NW
Washington, DC 20500
Visitors' Office: (202) 456-7041
http://www.whitehouse.gov

The Pierces lived in the White House from March 1853 to March 1857.

Online Sites of Interest

★ **Franklin Pierce**

http://www.franklinpierce.ws

A site established to observe the bicentennial of Pierce's birth in 2004. Provides a brief biography and information on the Pierce homestead.

★ **The American Presidency**

http://gi.grolier.com/presidents/preshome.html

Provides biographies of presidents at different reading levels. In addition, there are many features about the presidents, including election results and links to other sites.

★ **The White House**

www.whitehouse.gov/history/presidents/

Provides brief biographies of each president and first lady. In addition, there is much information about the White House itself and about the current administration.

★ **Internet Public Library: Presidents of the United States (IPL-POTUS)**

www.ipl.org/div/potus/fpierce.html

A site operated by the University of Michigan School of Information. Provides reliable information on the presidents and links to other sites.

★ **The American President**

http://www.americanpresident.org/history/

A site operated by the Miller Center at the University of Virginia. Provides useful information on each president's life, a timeline, and informative illustrations.

Table of Presidents

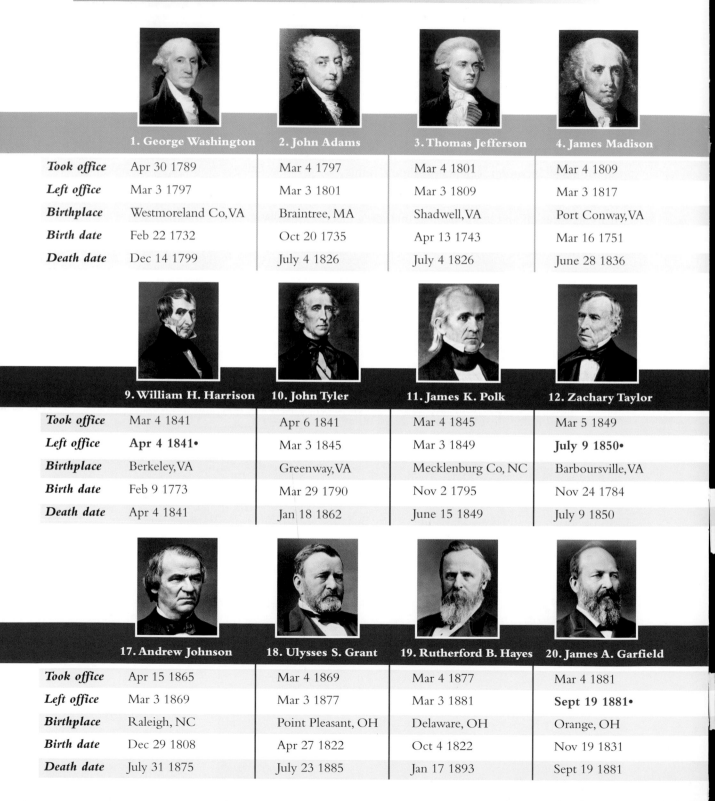

	1. George Washington	2. John Adams	3. Thomas Jefferson	4. James Madison
Took office	Apr 30 1789	Mar 4 1797	Mar 4 1801	Mar 4 1809
Left office	Mar 3 1797	Mar 3 1801	Mar 3 1809	Mar 3 1817
Birthplace	Westmoreland Co, VA	Braintree, MA	Shadwell, VA	Port Conway, VA
Birth date	Feb 22 1732	Oct 20 1735	Apr 13 1743	Mar 16 1751
Death date	Dec 14 1799	July 4 1826	July 4 1826	June 28 1836

	9. William H. Harrison	10. John Tyler	11. James K. Polk	12. Zachary Taylor
Took office	Mar 4 1841	Apr 6 1841	Mar 4 1845	Mar 5 1849
Left office	**Apr 4 1841•**	Mar 3 1845	Mar 3 1849	**July 9 1850•**
Birthplace	Berkeley, VA	Greenway, VA	Mecklenburg Co, NC	Barboursville, VA
Birth date	Feb 9 1773	Mar 29 1790	Nov 2 1795	Nov 24 1784
Death date	Apr 4 1841	Jan 18 1862	June 15 1849	July 9 1850

	17. Andrew Johnson	18. Ulysses S. Grant	19. Rutherford B. Hayes	20. James A. Garfield
Took office	Apr 15 1865	Mar 4 1869	Mar 4 1877	Mar 4 1881
Left office	Mar 3 1869	Mar 3 1877	Mar 3 1881	**Sept 19 1881•**
Birthplace	Raleigh, NC	Point Pleasant, OH	Delaware, OH	Orange, OH
Birth date	Dec 29 1808	Apr 27 1822	Oct 4 1822	Nov 19 1831
Death date	July 31 1875	July 23 1885	Jan 17 1893	Sept 19 1881

5. James Monroe	6. John Quincy Adams	7. Andrew Jackson	8. Martin Van Buren
Mar 4 1817	Mar 4 1825	Mar 4 1829	Mar 4 1837
Mar 3 1825	Mar 3 1829	Mar 3 1837	Mar 3 1841
Westmoreland Co, VA	Braintree, MA	The Waxhaws, SC	Kinderhook, NY
Apr 28 1758	July 11 1767	Mar 15 1767	Dec 5 1782
July 4 1831	Feb 23 1848	June 8 1845	July 24 1862

13. Millard Fillmore	14. Franklin Pierce	15. James Buchanan	16. Abraham Lincoln
July 9 1850	Mar 4 1853	Mar 4 1857	Mar 4 1861
Mar 3 1853	Mar 3 1857	Mar 3 1861	**Apr 15 1865•**
Locke Township, NY	Hillsborough, NH	Cove Gap, PA	Hardin Co, KY
Jan 7 1800	Nov 23 1804	Apr 23 1791	Feb 12 1809
Mar 8 1874	Oct 8 1869	June 1 1868	Apr 15 1865

21. Chester A. Arthur	22. Grover Cleveland	23. Benjamin Harrison	24. Grover Cleveland
Sept 19 1881	Mar 4 1885	Mar 4 1889	Mar 4 1893
Mar 3 1885	Mar 3 1889	Mar 3 1893	Mar 3 1897
Fairfield, VT	Caldwell, NJ	North Bend, OH	Caldwell, NJ
Oct 5 1830	Mar 18 1837	Aug 20 1833	Mar 18 1837
Nov 18 1886	June 24 1908	Mar 13 1901	June 24 1908

	25. William McKinley	26. Theodore Roosevelt	27. William H. Taft	28. Woodrow Wilson
Took office	Mar 4 1897	Sept 14 1901	Mar 4 1909	Mar 4 1913
Left office	**Sept 14 1901•**	Mar 3 1909	Mar 3 1913	Mar 3 1921
Birthplace	Niles, OH	New York, NY	Cincinnati, OH	Staunton, VA
Birth date	Jan 29 1843	Oct 27 1858	Sept 15 1857	Dec 28 1856
Death date	Sept 14 1901	Jan 6 1919	Mar 8 1930	Feb 3 1924

	33. Harry S. Truman	34. Dwight D. Eisenhower	35. John F. Kennedy	36. Lyndon B. Johnson
Took office	Apr 12 1945	Jan 20 1953	Jan 20 1961	Nov 22 1963
Left office	Jan 20 1953	Jan 20 1961	**Nov 22 1963•**	Jan 20 1969
Birthplace	Lamar, MO	Denison, TX	Brookline, MA	Johnson City, TX
Birth date	May 8 1884	Oct 14 1890	May 29 1917	Aug 27 1908
Death date	Dec 26 1972	Mar 28 1969	Nov 22 1963	Jan 22 1973

	41. George Bush	42. Bill Clinton	43. George W. Bush	
Took office	Jan 20 1989	Jan 20 1993	Jan 20 2001	
Left office	Jan 20 1993	Jan 20 2001	—	
Birthplace	Milton, MA	Hope, AR	New Haven, CT	
Birth date	June 12 1924	Aug 19 1946	July 6 1946	
Death date	—	—	—	

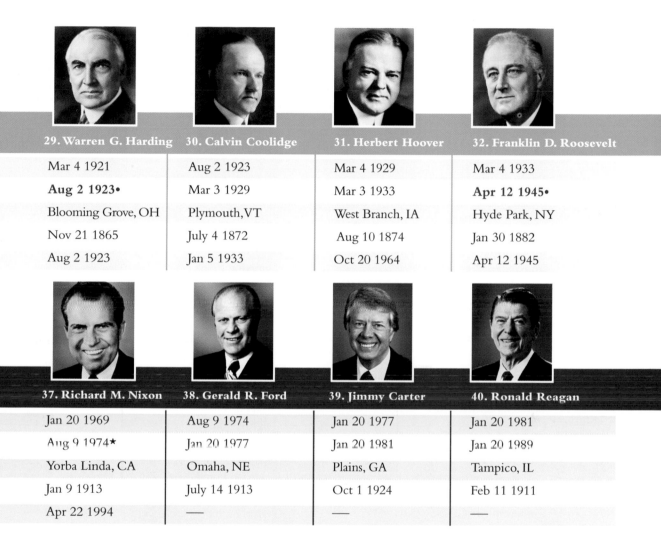

29. Warren G. Harding	30. Calvin Coolidge	31. Herbert Hoover	32. Franklin D. Roosevelt
Mar 4 1921	Aug 2 1923	Mar 4 1929	Mar 4 1933
Aug 2 1923•	Mar 3 1929	Mar 3 1933	**Apr 12 1945•**
Blooming Grove, OH	Plymouth, VT	West Branch, IA	Hyde Park, NY
Nov 21 1865	July 4 1872	Aug 10 1874	Jan 30 1882
Aug 2 1923	Jan 5 1933	Oct 20 1964	Apr 12 1945

37. Richard M. Nixon	38. Gerald R. Ford	39. Jimmy Carter	40. Ronald Reagan
Jan 20 1969	Aug 9 1974	Jan 20 1977	Jan 20 1981
Aug 9 1974★	Jan 20 1977	Jan 20 1981	Jan 20 1989
Yorba Linda, CA	Omaha, NE	Plains, GA	Tampico, IL
Jan 9 1913	July 14 1913	Oct 1 1924	Feb 11 1911
Apr 22 1994	—	—	—

• Indicates the president died while in office.

★ Richard Nixon resigned before his term expired.

Index

About the Author

John DiConsiglio is a writer in the Washington, D.C., area. He is the author of several books for young adults, including *Coming to America: Voices of Teenage Immigrants* (Scholastic, 2002). As a journalist, he has covered some of the top stories of the last decade, from presidential elections to Supreme Court decisions to the tragedy at Columbine High School. His work has appeared in numerous magazines including *People*, *Glamour*, *Redbook*, and *Cosmopolitan*. He is a graduate of Cornell University.